FIFTY
SHOES
THAT
CHANGED
THE
WORLD

**DESIGN
MUSEUM**

FIFTY
SHOES
THAT
CHANGED
THE
WORLD

conran
OCTOPUS

FIFTY
SHOES

FIFTY
SHOES

It is remarkable how rapidly the shoe has evolved in the past few decades. The trainer, or sneaker, has transformed what we understand as everyday footwear, creating a clear barrier between generations – much to the despair of drill sergeants, who encounter recruits with feet unable to adapt to the constraints of wearing boots. New materials, fixings, ways of waterproofing, and so on have changed many of the basic parameters. Nonetheless, for all the shoe's mercurial, polymorphous nature, there are archetypes that have managed to migrate from the past into new forms of footwear. Closely related to the fashion industry, the shoe continues, too, to span both industrial mass production and individual handcraft making.

The shoe clearly exerts a fascination on the popular imagination. In 20 years of temporary exhibitions at the Design Museum, the retrospective on Manolo Blahnik staged in 2003 – at the very height of the *Sex and the City* phenomenon – still holds the record for the exhibition that attracted more visitors in any one week than any other.

This selection of 50 designs explores the full range of shoe design, showing how footwear can address both comfort and self-image, fashion and technology.

Deyan Sudjic, Director, Design Museum

Right: Looking into the heel of the Electric Light Shoe, a metre-long sculpture produced as part of the 2008 Electric Tiger Land marketing campaign to promote Onitsuka Tiger, the Japanese shoe brand.

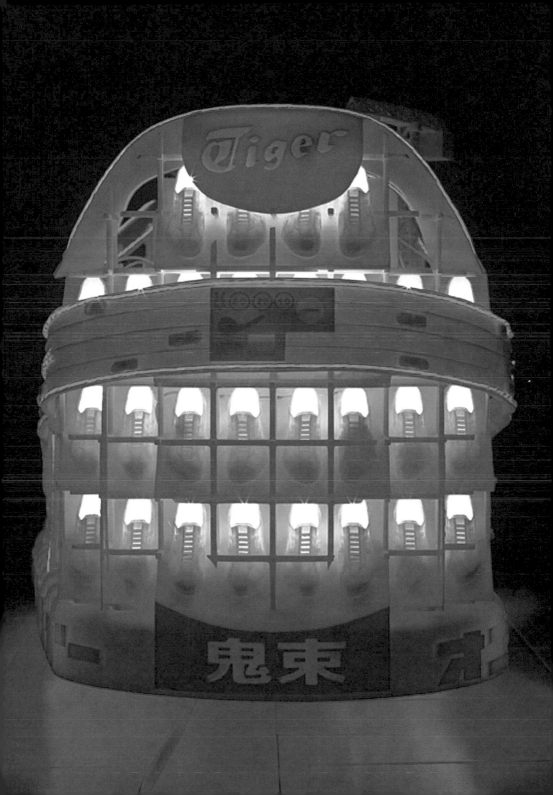

PLIMSOLL

1830s
Liverpool Rubber
Company (later Dunlop)

There was once a casual shoe that dominated the sporting world and filled every school gymnasium with sliding squeaks and the smell of rubber. The forerunner of the trainer, and the instigator of the cultural phenomenon of dressing down in comfortable sporty footwear, the plimsoll had various moments of supremacy from the 1830s until quite late into the twentieth century.

This unpretentious shoe was first worn by the British working classes while holidaying by the sea. Early manifestations of these 'sand shoes' had leather or rope soles and canvas uppers. The rubber-soled version appeared in the 1830s, produced by the Liverpool Rubber Company (later to become Dunlop). Another improvement was the thick band of rubber that circled the shoe to strengthen and protect the join between rubber sole and canvas top. It was this band, said to resemble the Plimsoll line around the hull of a ship, that gave the shoe its name in the late nineteenth century, at least in Britain. In the United States the plimsoll is generally known as a tennis shoe or sneaker.

Shock-absorbing and kind to lawns, the plimsoll fast became a favourite sporting shoe and was widely adopted by athletes at the 1924 Paris Olympics.

Right: The mass-manufactured iconic plimsoll at various stages of production. It evolved into a mainstay sports shoe, widely used through the nineteenth and twentieth centuries.

GALOSH

The definition of a 'galosh' is a covering worn over more vulnerable indoor shoes to protect them from wet and muddy outdoor conditions. Early and ancient versions would have consisted of a thick wooden sole topped with either a mule-type shoe into which to slip the foot or a sleeve of weatherproofed fabric or leather fastened around the lower leg.

The word itself suggests the antiquity of the idea: 'galosh' is thought to derive from the Latin term *gallica solea* – 'Gallic shoe' – used by the Romans to describe the rugged wooden-soled boots worn by the warriors of Gaul (modern France). In Victorian times, or so the story goes, the idea was taken up by a rheumatic Englishman who read about the overshoes in Julius Caesar's account of his campaigns in Gaul and wanted to protect his own feet from the damp.

In reality, it seems, the galosh was pulled into the modern age by the American entrepreneur Charles Goodyear (1800–60), who in 1839 discovered the process of vulcanization that renders rubber tougher and more resistant to extreme conditions. As in every other field of design, new technologies were to revolutionize shoes and their production.

Right: Fashionably dressed young women wear galoshes to protect their smart shoes from the dirt of the street.

FRYE BOOT

The Frye Company was founded in the United States by an English immigrant bootmaker, John A Frye (died 1911), in 1863 and is today one of the country's oldest surviving footwear manufacturers. Worn by both Confederate and Union soldiers during the American Civil War, and by many of the pioneers who colonized the West through the late nineteenth century, Frye boots are closely entwined with the country's history. Later, in the twentieth century, Frye's classic harness boots would become a favourite among US servicemen in World War II.

The first pair of Frye's was 'bench crafted' in 1863, and the boots are still made to this day with the same attention to detail – the company proudly claims that there are 190 steps in the construction of a single boot. An emblem of continuity, quality and, some might add, old-fashioned machismo, the Frye boot is a nostalgia-laden survivor from a time when the American nation was still being forged. As living history, the boot has lasted the test of time and is still popular today thanks to a successful 1960s reissue of the 1860s original.

Right: The Frye boot in action – Alfred R Waud, intrepid artist correspondent for *Harper's Weekly* magazine, sketches the Gettysburg battlefield in 1863. Below: The Frye boot is as old as the modern United States and for many symbolizes the country's turbulent history as well as its rugged landscape.

SPECTATOR SHOE

1868
John Lobb

The spectator shoe is a dressy item of footwear that has had various manifestations from the mid nineteenth century onwards. An early example is attributed to the London bespoke bootmaker John Lobb (1829–95), who created two-toned gentlemen's cricket shoes in 1868. The originals would most probably have had a white body, with a brown or black toe and heel, but there have been variations in colour across the many reinterpretations of this basic design over the years. Original materials would have included brown willow calf and white buck. With comfort and practicability in mind, the toe area sometimes had broguing to ventilate the shoe in hot weather.

The spectator emerged at a time of increased leisure activity and informality among the fashionable classes. Popularity was ensured when the trendsetting, debonair Duke of Windsor sported a spiked pair when playing golf. Away from sporting pursuits, the shoe became a gesture of informality to accompany a day suit in the 1920s and 1930s, and the design also filtered into women's fashion of the time.

Close-fitting, comfortable and flexible, it also became the perfect footwear for the Jazz Age dance floor. In Hollywood films the two-toned spectator became a trademark of the elegant king of the dance floor, Fred Astaire.

Right: James Cagney and Sophia Delza stepping out on stage in the Broadway show *The Grand Street Follies of 1928*. Cagney is sporting an especially dapper pair of spectator shoes – the perfect way to cut a dash in the 1920s and 1930s.

ALL-STAR BASKETBALL SHOE   1917
Converse

All sizes and all colours, but only one classic shape that has managed to stand the test of time for nearly a century. The All-Star basketball shoe was created by the Converse Rubber Corporation and originated in Massachusetts in 1917.

In 1921, in a now all-too-familiar example of sports personality endorsement, Converse hired the basketball star Charles 'Chuck' H Taylor to promote the shoe, and two years later the 'Chuck Taylor' name began to appear on every ankle patch. 'Cons' or 'Chuckers', as they quickly came to be dubbed, were now well on their way to becoming a household name. Initially the canvas-and-rubber All-Stars came in just one colour – a utilitarian black – but in the 1960s, under pressure from the nation's fiercely competitive basketball teams, Converse began to introduce an array of others.

The All-Star has long since strayed from the basketball pitch and now stands as one of the most iconic and versatile examples of twentieth-century footwear design. Rock and grunge no longer have a monopoly – whether worn with jeans or accessorizing a suit, the shoe's status transcends fashion categories and genres.

Right: The Ramones in 1977 wearing Converse All-Stars in one cool manifestation of the long-lived sporty shoe. Below: Andy Warhol portrayed this American icon in his painting *Converse Extra Special Value* (1985–6).

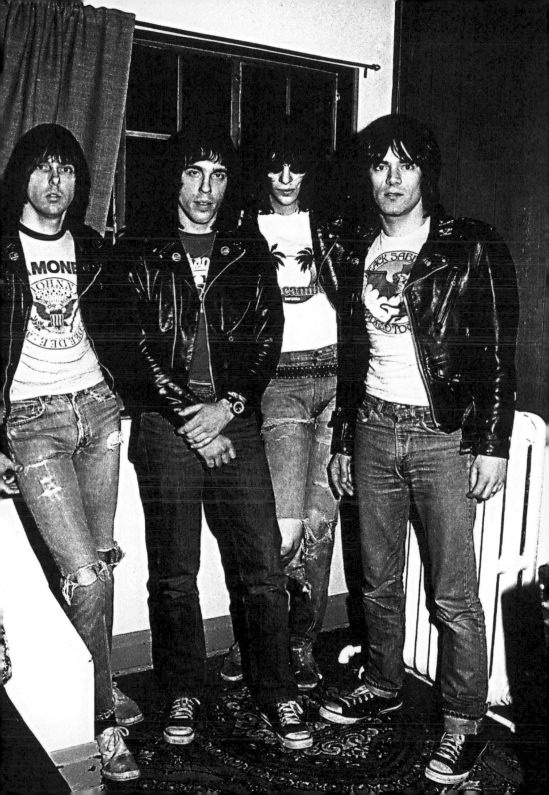

LACED SHOE WITH PATCHWORK UPPER

Salvatore Ferragamo (1898–1960) was among the greatest and most gifted shoe designers of the twentieth century, responsible for the creation of exuberant, innovative designs that have proved irresistible to generations of wealthy women – from Hollywood to Bollywood and the occasional spouse of a dictator. Ferragamo could produce extravagant one-offs such as a pair of 18-carat gold sandals made in 1956; patented innovations such as the cork wedge heel (1937; see pages 22–3) and enduring classics such as the Invisible sandal (1947).

In a rags-to-riches story that could have been written as a fairytale, Ferragamo began making shoes at the age of nine. By the age of 14, he had set up shop in his parents' house in Bonito, southern Italy, and two years later he emigrated to the United States where he rapidly forged his reputation among the Hollywood good and great. Although he would eventually return to Italy in 1927, he retained a loyal clientele among the Tinseltown stars. Thus he created more than forty pairs of shoes for Marilyn Monroe, including the pair of slingback sandals she wore for the legendary 'subway grate' scene in *The Seven Year Itch* (1955).

This beautiful laced shoe with patchwork upper dates from the period immediately following Ferragamo's return to Italy, when he opened a workshop and shop in Florence.

Right: This elegant patchwork shoe is a fine example of the beautifully crafted work of Italian designer Salvatore Ferragamo. Patchwork would be an enduring theme in the shoe designer's work.

MA GOUVERNANTE

Shoes have been the objects of fetishistic desire in various periods and in different cultures. In twentieth-century Modernist art, an early response to what is sometimes known as retifism is one of the best-known pieces by the Swiss Surrealist artist and photographer Méret Oppenheim (1913–85) – the sculpture *Ma gouvernante* (*My Governness*; sometimes known as My Nurse).

Both witty and troubling, Oppenheim's 'object' consists of a pair of high-heeled white leather shoes trussed together and turned upside down on a platter. Completing the collision between – and elision of – fashion, food and sexuality are the paper chop frills decorating the upturned heels. Most of the Surrealists shared an obsession with the female body, but Oppenheim brought her own feminist perspective to their concerns, revealing the hidden sadism that, in Freudian and Jungian thought, can underpin male heterosexual desire.

Fashion, sex and oppression have never been far apart, but here the whole conundrum is tied up in a single unsettling image.

Right: Shoes as fetish – the Surrealist artist Méret Oppenheim explores the links between fashion, sexuality and the 'sex war' in her 1936 sculpture *Ma gouvernante*.

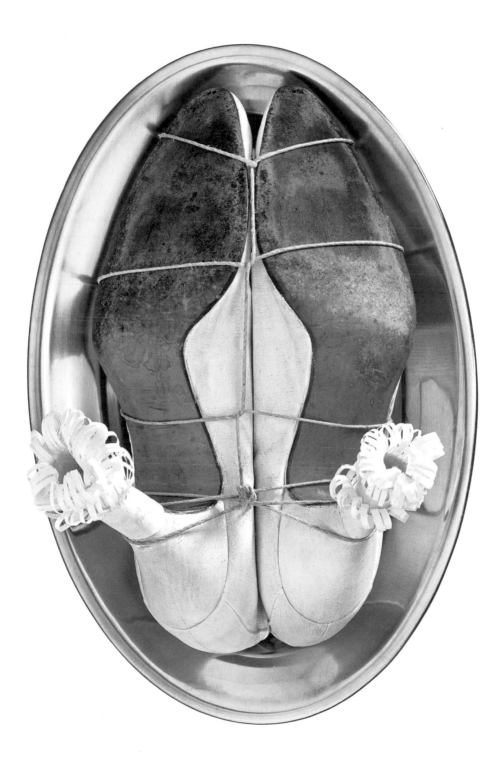

CARMEN MIRANDA'S PLATFORM SHOE

1938
Salvatore Ferragamo

During the mid-1930s the Italian designer Salvatore Ferragamo began to experiment with cork platform soles. Platform shoes, of course, have an ancient history, often worn as a practical way of keeping the wearer's feet out of the muck of the street. During the 1930s, however, the platform emerged as a fashion item – an ideal way to elongate the figure while wearing an elegant floor-length dress or fluid wide-bottomed trousers.

In Ferragamo's case, there was a practical motivation for his interest in the platform – in 1935 the Italian dictator Mussolini ordered the invasion of Ethiopia and the League of Nations imposed an economic embargo on Italy that led to a critical shortage of materials. Resourceful as ever, Ferragamo used wine corks to create a lightweight yet sturdy base for a shoe, which could then be covered with material such as leather to disguise its origins. He took out a patent on this construction method in 1937 – the first patent in the history of fashion.

Ferragamo's platforms were widely sought after. In 1938 he created a gorgeous pair of multicoloured suede platforms for the actress Judy Garland as well as an intricately patterned pair for Indira, Maharani of Cooch Beh, and, in the following year, these glittering shoes for Carmen Miranda. Although Ferragamo's business skills could be shaky, by the time of his death in 1960 his workshops employed some 750 artisans producing 350 handmade shoes a day. Today Ferragamo continues to thrive as an international luxury brand. The platform, too, lives on (see pages 52–3 and 64–5).

Right: These glittering shoes were made by Salvatore Ferragamo for samba singer Carmen Miranda at the height of the platform's popularity in the 1930s. The gilded-glass mosaic platform is topped by an upper of black silk and gold kid.

DOROTHY'S RUBY SLIPPERS

1939
Adrian

What happens when freak weather conditions hurl your house into a chromatically intense world of Munchkins and mayhem and you inadvertently squash to death a tyrannical, hook-nosed witch? In Dorothy's case, she got a fantastic pair of sparkly new crimson shoes. Her Ruby Slippers immediately became an iconic image when the film *The Wizard of Oz* was released in 1939 – a gorgeous symbol of the American Dream and a reminder that 'there's no place like home'.

However, the magic red slippers were an MGM invention, replacing the original silver shoes that L Frank Baum, author of *The Wonderful Wizard of Oz* (1900), originally described. The choice was a practical one – red showed up so much better than silver in Technicolor, the richly chromatic film stock that the film helped pioneer. The shoes were created by MGM costume designer Adrian (Adrian Adolph Greenberg, 1903–59), who transformed ordinary pairs of white silk pumps by covering them with burgundy-sequinned organza and adding extravagant bows studded with bugle beads and glass rhinestones. Four pairs of the fabulous Ruby Slippers survive today.

Dorothy's sparkly slippers tap into every girl's and woman's joy in dressing up. The right shoes can make you feel empowered, can get you noticed … can be magic.

Right: Click your heels three times … Dorothy's Ruby Slippers are a cinematic icon and an enduring symbol of the American Dream. Below: Dorothy and her companions dance their way along the Yellow Brick Road in *The Wizard of Oz*.

SLINGBACK SANDAL

The slingback first emerged as a fashionable shoe in the 1930s and has been revisited by both haute-couture designers and mainstream manufacturers ever since. A practical benefit that makes this style so desirable is that it can be slipped easily onto the foot without the need for fiddling with either strap or buckle. The strap anchors the shoe to the foot, allowing for the minimum of material to be used in the shoe upper, and leaving the heel and ankle exposed. This is a shoe in which the foot itself is an integral part of the visual effect, and it's a style that lends itself well to both casual and dressy occasions.

The strappy upper means that the mouldable properties of leather are not necessarily required and a variety of other materials can be used instead. This British-made slingback sandal from the 1940s is a good early example of a synthetic material being used in a mass-manufactured shoe. This would have been particularly poignant at a time when wartime and postwar shortages placed draconian restrictions on fashion design.

Right: The slingback has been a fashion mainstay since it first emerged in the 1930s. These 1940s slingback sandals are an example of synthetic materials being used creatively in a mass-manufactured shoe.

THE 'DOC MARTENS' SHOE

1947
Klaus Märtens

The Dr Martens shoe is a staple of classic British street style and has been an iconic brand for the country's youth subcultures since the late 1960s. For skinheads and, later, the punks, the sturdy, no-nonsense Doc Martens, or 'DMs', sent out a message of defiance and aggression, signalling an appropriation of masculine working-class garb and culture in an era of economic and social upheaval. For some, the number of eyelets and the colour of the laces could become objects of near-fetishistic obsession.

The origins of this seemingly archetypal British footwear lie, however, in Germany. In 1945 the German army physician Klaus Märtens suffered an ankle injury during a skiing trip in the Bavarian Alps and came up with the idea of using soles of air-impregnated rubber to offer wearers both comfort and support. In 1947 Märtens, in pursuit of his venture, teamed up with an old university friend, Dr Herbert Funck, to manufacture the shoe and their product became an immediate hit. Oddly perhaps, given the brand's subsequent history, it sold especially well to Germany's hard-pressed housewives.

Right and below: Dr Klaus Märtens's innovative boots and shoes have become a staple of street style around the world.

DESERT BOOT

Since its first appearance in 1949, the Desert boot has become an icon synonymous with several generations of hip youth culture. A comfortable blend of elegant styling and relaxed, floppy cosiness, this boot met the rapidly evolving fashion trends of the postwar era, as teenagers increasingly laid claim to a distinct social and visual identity.

The original Desert boot was produced by C J Clark, the British family-run shoe manufacturer, better known simply as Clarks. It was devised by Nathan Clark, who based the design on a popular boot that his fellow British Army officers had had made for themselves in Cairo's Khan el-Khalili bazaar. The thin crepe sole took advantage of new synthetic materials and manufacturing processes, while mass production was made possible by the company's expansion into a number of new factories.

In an otherwise traditional shoe market, the Desert boot struck a radical note. The design, however, has mellowed with age and today exudes an understated neutrality that will ensure its continued longevity. In 2009 Clarks launched a fiftieth-anniversary celebration of the Desert boot, with an eclectic new design for every decade, encompassing unconventional paisley prints, denim and tweed.

Right: From hip footwear to mellow understatement – the classic Desert boot helped to establish the Clarks brand in postwar Britain.

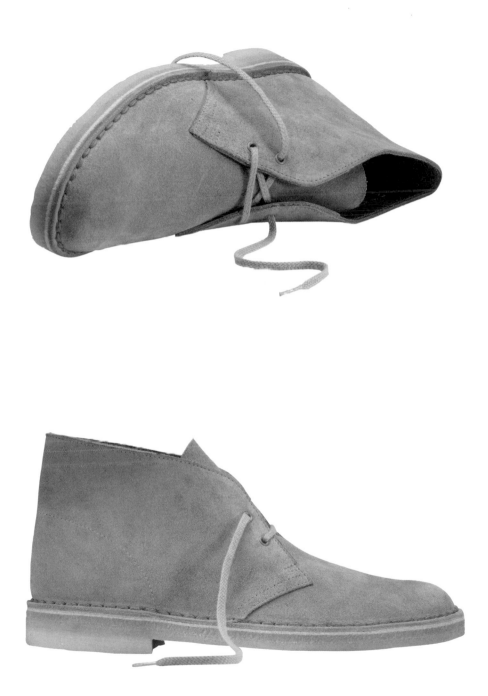

STILETTO

The word 'stiletto' is derived from the Latin *stilus*, which means a pin or stake. During the Renaissance it was the name given to a thin-bladed weapon, the archetypal tool of trade of the 'cloak-and-dagger' assassin … an apt parallel, perhaps, with the piercingly pointed shoe heel that emerged after World War II, the must-have apparel of every self-respecting *femme fatale*.

Stiletto-style heels can be dated back to at least the eighteenth century, but they were reformulated in the late 1950s by the French designer Roger Vivier (1907–98), who gave them their modern name. To maximize the slenderness, height and strength of his opulent shoes, Vivier encased a thin steel rod within a wooden or plastic heel. The optical effect was to lengthen and attenuate the wearer's legs and to emphasize her buttocks and bust; the *actual* effect, of course, was to stop men in their tracks.

In the age-old battle of the sexes, the stiletto is as potent a weapon as the dagger it is named after. Rather than objectifying the wearer, the stiletto's proselytizers claim, they empower her – whether for boardroom or for bedroom warfare. As the object of fetishistic desire, moreover, the stiletto is undoubtedly a masochist's dream. These shoes were made for walking, and walking right over men.

Right: The stiletto is the epitome of the sexy shoe. Sigmund Freud would have a field day with these piercing, slender heels.

THE 'CENDRILLON' BALLET SHOE

1956
Rose Repetto

The ballet shoe danced its way from stage to street in typically fairytale fashion. The curtain rose in 1947 when, in a tiny Parisian workshop, Rose Repetto crafted a pair of pointes for her son, Roland Petit, the renowned dancer and choreographer. The shoes' unusual comfort made them an instant hit with Roland and it wasn't long before Repetto shoes became the favoured footwear of dancers and ballet companies around the world.

However, the leap from stage to high fashion came in 1956 when the young Brigitte Bardot asked Rose Repetto to make a pair of ballet slippers for her to wear in Roger Vadim's film *Et Dieu … créea la femme* (*And God Created Woman*). The red Cendrillon ballerinas, named after the French version of Cinderella, were lightweight and comfortable, but sexy, too – perfect for the kittenish teenage character played by Bardot in the film. Vadim's erotic drama was a popular success and so were the shoes, which went into commercial production soon afterwards.

Offering simple streamlined comfort with a hint of the romance and glamour of the prima ballerina, the shoes have continued in production until the present day. More recently the well-known fashion label Comme des Garçons has helped to reinvigorate the star of the Repetto fashion line.

Right: Brigitte Bardot launches her career in the film *And God Created Woman* (1956) sporting a pair of Repetto ballet shoes. The specially designed red shoes were an enormous commercial hit when the film came out.

CURD JÜRGENS · BRIGITTE BARDOT
**Und immer lockt
das Weib**
EIN COLUMBIA-FARBFILM IN
CinemaScope
FARBE VON EASTMANCOLOR

HUSH PUPPIES 1958

Bastions of casual comfort, Hush Puppies first appeared in the United States in 1958 and quickly became *the* masculine shoe of suburbia. New attitudes to leisure and a new, more compartmentalized way of living required a rethink about how men dressed outside the workplace. Until this point men's shoes were not relaxed unless they were sporty or for holidaywear. What Hush Puppies made possible was an informal look that did not compromise on either style or seriousness.

The brand name derived from the Southern dish of fried cornballs that were supposedly thrown to barking dogs to quieten them. The name perfectly summed up the shoe's homely style, with its combination of supple suede upper and lightweight crepe sole. The company logo – a sleepy-eyed basset hound – pressed home the brand's snug domesticity.

It was this same unsexy cosiness that doubtlessly led to the near-demise of Hush Puppies in the 1990s, by which time the 'casual' shoe as a concept had been largely displaced by the athletic shoe, or trainer. However, Hush Puppies had an unexpected renaissance, first re-emerging as a 'hip', retro style in Manhattan's clubs and bars. For cultural commentator Malcolm Gladwell, this phenomenon was a textbook example of the viral nature of modern capitalist culture.

Right and below: With their suede uppers and crepe soles, Hush Puppies have traditionally suggested homely comfort. More recently, the brand has acquired a kind of retro chic.

CHELSEA BOOT

While women's fashion in the 1960s indulged in futuristic fantasy, men's fashion was redefining traditionalism with reinterpretations of the suit and the emergence of the classic 'Chelsea boot'. This laceless, ankle-high boot with its elastic gusset provided sleek old-school modernity for Britain's Mods – the bespoke-tailored, amphetamine-fuelled denizens of Britain's cappuccino bars and dancing clubs. Modelled by youth icons from the Beatles to the Stones, this was the footwear to be seen in if you wanted to be 'hip' and 'sharp'.

With the same fervour of appropriation that gave Rockers their 'Edwardian' jackets, the Mods chose a boot that originated in a previous era. The Chelsea boot is a modern version of the nineteenth-century jodhpur (or paddock) boot. Named after the former capital of the Indian state of Rajasthan, the boot was initially marketed as a riding boot for British colonials. The gusset made of elastic vulcanized rubber made the boot easy to pull on and off and provided heightened ankle support with no need for laces.

Today the Chelsea has classic status in the stylish contemporary man's wardrobe. Who knows, though? If the white-sprayed Chelseas worn by the Empire's stormtroopers in the *Star Wars* sequence are anything to go by, perhaps it's the shoe of the future, too!

Right: The elastic gusset gave the Chelsea boot a streamlined modernity eagerly adopted by Mods in the early 1960s. In all probability, they would have been unaware of the shoe's nineteenth-century colonial origins.

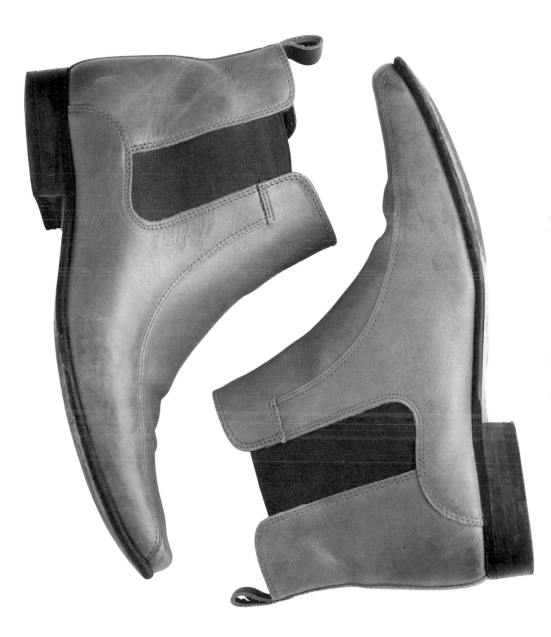

EIGHT-EYELET BOOT

By the late 1950s Dr Märtens and Dr Funck's sturdy, utilitarian boot (see pages 28–9) had more than proved its popularity in West Germany and they were ready to launch their footwear internationally. In Britain they sold the patent to the traditional Northamptonshire shoe company R Griggs, which launched its first 'Dr Martens' in 1960 – an oxblood-red, eight-eyelet boot marketed under the unassuming name of 'the 1460'.

Griggs had not only anglicized the name (excising the foreign-looking umlaut); it also altered the heel, added distinctive yellow stitching and trademarked the cushioned rubber soles under the name AirWair. It was a look that would brand the Dr Martens aesthetic onto the public consciousness. Its sturdy comfort meant the eight-eyelet boot was initially popular among postmen and police officers, but over time it was also adopted as a uniform by various subcultures and it became the footwear of insouciant, rebellious youth.

Swinging between counterculture and mainstream, this domesticated military boot has been appropriated by a succession of gritty urban tribes. Young or old, dapper or dorky, straight or gay, the 1460 has been the proclaimer of anti-establishment individuality for more than forty years.

Right: Not just for the boys – bright and colourful interpretations of the DM boot worn by two young and groovy girls. Below: The oxblood-red uppers and robust yellow stitching are indispensable elements of this iconic boot.

PLASTIC KNEE-HIGH BOOTS

1960s
Mary Quant

The British designer Mary Quant (1934–), of course, is most closely associated with the miniskirt, the archetypal garment of the Swinging Sixties. By the middle of that decade, the Quant look was at its height, with the designer marketing a full range of accessories – including patent-plastic raincoats, underwear, 'paintbox' cosmetics, underwear and footwear – from her King's Road and Knightsbridge shops in London. This was the Space Age style at its most sexy, fun and liberating.

The knee-high boot was the ideal complement to the mini, providing a perfect balance to the upwardly mobile hemline. The shiny, machine-moulded plastic was an uninhibited gesture towards modernity, while the zipper ran not only down the length of the boot but also around the ankle, so the top part could be completely detached. The square toe was another feature favoured by Quant at this time.

Right and below: Mary Quant's Space Age plastic boots fitted perfectly into the new pop look that gave young women a new identity in the 1960s. The five-petalled daisy was Quant's logo, found on the base of the boot's heel as well as in this promotional photo.

WINKLEPICKERS

There is a quaint British seaside tradition of eating 'winkles' – periwinkle snails – from paper bags, using a pin – or 'winklepicker' – to extract the mollusc from its shell, and it is this that gave the exaggeratedly pointed men's shoe of post-World War II Britain its name. There was a fashion for wearing pointed shoes, or *poulaines*, among Europe's elite in medieval times, but the modern winklepicker first emerged in the 1920s and 1930s. It was not until the 1950s, though, that it really came into its own as an optional addition to the Teddy Boy uniform.

As street styles evolved, a new wave of quiffed Rockers abandoned the shoe in favour of more robust urban footwear and the winklepicker was adopted instead by the smooth-haired, Italian-suited Mods (see pages 38–9). This was the perfect shoe with which to cut through the air while zipping through town on a Vespa, *dolce vita*–style. Media frenzy around gang fights between Mods and Rockers suggested that the pointed shoe was used as a weapon but in reality it seems unlikely that the image-concious Mods would have subjected their expensive footwear to such misuse.

The heyday of the winklepicker was short and sweet, though the style has resurfaced from time to time. Currently, a new generation has adopted the footwear and winklepickers are strutted by a host of bands from garage rockers the Horrors to post-punks Neils Children.

Right: The sleek, pointy winklepicker was a key part of the cool look for Mods, both men and women.

FLIP-FLOP

Cheap to make and buy and easy to wear, rubber flip-flops are the footwear of our childhood holidays. Who can forget the feel of sun-baked rubber on their feet or the irritating rub of the strap between the big and index toes? For millions of people in developing countries around the world, however, they are simply the only affordable shoes.

For all their ubiquity, flip-flops have a distinguished pedigree, ultimately stretching back, it seems, to the Japanese rice-straw sandals known as *zori*. The credit for their development into mass-market footwear is much disputed, but adapted rubber versions seem first to have appeared in New Zealand in the 1950s, or perhaps even earlier, and were commonly known as 'jandals' – short for 'Japanese sandals'.

Very quickly, versions of the jandal began to be manufactured around the globe. Havaianas, for instance, was a brand first produced in Brazil in the early 1960s, and was the ideal footwear to exploit that country's abundant supply of rubber. Havaianas took their name from the Portuguese for the beach-loving Hawaiians; in the UK and United States the sandals were onomatopoeically and affectionately nicknamed 'flip-flops'.

Colourful, bouncy and fun, flip-flops are not a shoe for everyday use, but are perfect beachwear and the only footwear conceivable on sunny summer days.

Right: Havaiana flip-flops – informal footwear perfect for a balmy beach vacation. Generally cheap to buy and sand- and water-friendly, flip-flops are synonymous with getting away from it all.

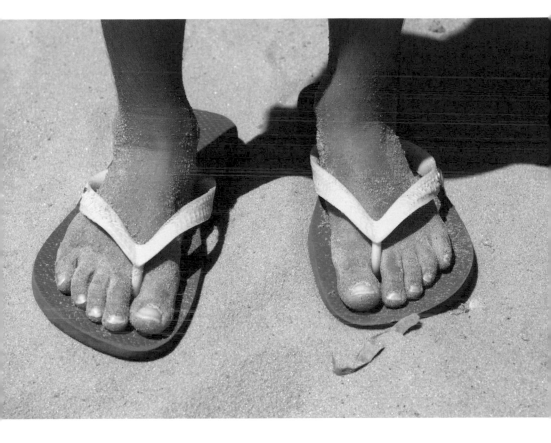

DRIVING SHOE

An Italian design that perfectly encapsulates the American Dream, the Tod's driving shoe is a powerful understatement of success, its clean-cut, pared-down quality an epitome of the comfort and luxury of contemporary middle-class living.

The modern luxury-goods brand Tod's has its origins in a small Italian shoemaking business founded by Filippo Della Vale in the 1900s. In the 1980s Filippo's ambitious grandson, Diego Della Valle (1953–), moved to New York City, set up a temporary showroom in his hotel bedroom, and was soon selling his family's beautiful handmade shoes to US department stores such as Bloomingdale's. In 1987 Della Valle launched his own Manhattan store, whose all-American name, J P Tod's, he picked out of a New York telephone directory.

Pride of place in the J P Tod's store was given to the company's luxurious driving shoe – a kid-soft moccasin first introduced by Della Valle in Italy in the 1970s. Very quickly the Gommino – named for the 133 rubber pebbles, or studs, on its sole and heel that help stop feet from sliding off car pedals when driving – eclipsed the rest of the Della Valle range and it has remained at the heart of the business ever since, for all the company's other luxurious innovations.

Made from just two beautifully crafted pieces of leather, the Tod's driving shoe is an exquisite blend of masculine practicality and feminine softness – just perfect for that lazy weekend drive down New York's Park Avenue.

Right: Comfort and luxury – the classic Tod's driving shoe in a variety of eye-catching colours. Below: The simple, pull-on style makes the shoe a favourite for urban relaxation – in or out of the car.

'OSSIE' SHOE

1972
Manolo Blahnik

As British *Vogue* editor Alexandra Shulman once quipped, 'If God had wanted us to wear flat shoes, he wouldn't have invented Manolo Blahnik.' The near-idolatrous position occupied by Blahnik in contemporary fashion reached a peak in recent years when his shoes became the coveted favourites of Carrie Bradshaw in *Sex and the City* (see pages 68–9). However, the path to this apotheosis had begun much earlier, in the early 1970s, with his association with the maverick British designer Ossie Clark (1942–96).

The son of wealthy parents, Blahnik (1942–) grew up in the Canary Islands then moved to London in the late 1960s, after a stint studying art in Paris. His early efforts at couture were dismissed out of hand by Diana Vreeland, the editor of US *Vogue*, who recommended he try shoe design instead. Basing himself at a shop in London's fashionable Chelsea, Blahnik initially focused on designing men's shoes but he quickly found the restricting conventions of that discipline frustrating. His big break came in 1972 when Clark invited Blahnik to produce the shoes to accompany his next collection.

Blahnik's flamboyant, experimental designs were the perfect match for Clark's couture. However, his imaginative flair was – as yet – untempered by technical know-how, and the teetering shoes proved perilous to wear – 'like walking on quicksand', Blahnik later recalled. Their visual bravura drew plaudits nevertheless, and the designer, an inveterate socialite, found himself lionized. In 1974 he garnered the distinction of becoming the first man to appear on the cover of British *Vogue*.

Right: Manolo Blahnik's sketch for one of the fanciful shoes that accompanied Ossie Clark's 1972 couture collection. Clark helped launch Blahnik as one of the most exciting and sought-after shoe designers of recent years.

Cherry Shoe made in 3 colour/black

David Baddeley Ossie Clark
London 1972. Right continues...

PLATFORM SHOES

In the early 1970s Biba, the fashion label launched by Polish-born Barbara Hulanicki (1936–) and her late husband, was at the height of its popularity, promoting a youthful, moody look of smocks, strong make-up and flamboyant platform shoes. Leapfrogging from mail-order business to boutique to grandiose department store, this image-conscious retailer provoked a frenzy among London's young and trendy. If you were going to buy the right pair of platform shoes, this was the place to go.

Many Biba designs harked back to the Art Deco fashions of the 1930s, and it was no wonder that the 'Biba Look' adopted the platform, too (see pages 22–3). By this time the 1970s revival of the platform had already begun, but, in comparison with its 1930s counterpart, the style was often much more ostentatious, becoming closely associated with the show-stopping antics of glam rockers and the disco-stomping kitsch of Abba. By the middle of the decade the platforms had grown to outlandish proportions and had little to recommend them except as an unsubtle means of attracting attention.

Dating from the beginning of the vogue, these Biba platforms recaptured something of the elegance of their 1930s forebears, however. The design is well balanced and harmonious, while the zigzag pattern covering upper, platform and heel is zany without being outrageous. With its consummate eye, Biba had caught a style before the tide rose too high.

Right: The platform shoe was resurrected in the 1970s to become synonymous with the glam-rock style of the time. These beautiful shoes by London retailer Biba, however, spell flamboyance tempered by restraint.

TIMBERLAND BOOT

1973

The very word Timberland conjures up images of the rugged all-American hunk, clad in check shirt, blue jeans and no-nonsense footwear. Pull on a pair of 'Timbos' and you feel ready to face even the bleakest wilderness, even if it just an urban street.

Although the company today manufactures a wide range of outdoor apparel, boots have always been at the heart of the business. Founded as the Abington Shoe Company in 1933, the Boston-based enterprise began to expand rapidly in the 1950s under the aegis of shoe stitcher made good Nathan Swartz and his sons. In 1973 Abington launched a waterproof boot branded the Timberland, which proved so popular that the company decided to rename itself to capitalize on its success.

The numerous versions of the waterproof boot issued in subsequent decades have not strayed far from the original. With its thick soles and robust stitching, chunky outline and stripped-back, earth-hue form, the Timberland appears to be almost a pastiche of the sturdy boot. While its essence may not have changed, however, its popularity has taken it far indeed from the forests and mountains for which it was designed. The Timberland is now primarily a fashion item, a statement of American outdoorsiness aimed primarily at the urban gaze. As ever in design, 'lifestyle' should never be confused with real life.

Right and below: The Timberland is the all-American boot – symbol of the great outdoors and the gritty urban street.

WAFFLE TRAINER

1974
Blue Ribbon Sports/Nike

The Waffle trainer was undoubtedly the most decisive shoe in the history of Nike, Inc., launching the company along its trajectory to becoming a global leader in innovative and desirable athletic footwear. This was before Nike was Nike. Blue Ribbon Sports was founded in Eugene, Oregon, USA in 1964, as a distributor for running shoes produced by Onitsuka Tiger (see pages 98–9). One of its founders was the University of Oregon track and field coach, Bill Bowerman (1911–99), who – apart from waxing lyrical on the virtues of jogging – spent most of his time designing running shoes and experimenting with new materials to improve both grip and speed.

In around 1970–71 Bowerman developed a lightweight, gridlike sole after testing out liquid polyurethane in his wife's waffle iron and this eventually led to the launch of the Waffle trainer in 1974, the company's first national bestseller. Its success was doubly assured when the US tennis star Jimmy Connors won the Wimbledon men's final wearing Waffles that same year.

Nike became Nike legally in 1978, but by then the company was on the fast track to world domination – thanks, in large part, to the Waffle.

Right: It sounds like an urban legend, but Bill Bowerman first developed this shoe while experimenting with a household waffle iron. Nike capitalized on the story in its promotional literature (below).

NIKE WAFFLES MAKE FOOTWEAR NEWS.

UGG BOOT

The history of this traditional Australian boot long precedes its recent global brand success – versions of the ugg are said to have been around for two hundred years, offering comfort and warmth to generations of Aussie settlers. The term 'ugg boots' has been used as a generic description for sheepskin boots in Australia since the mid twentieth century – supposedly because of their 'ugly' or homely appearance.

The thermostatic properties of sheepskin mean that uggs are warming in winter but also cooling in summer. This versatility made them a year-round footwear choice, and in the 1960s they were adopted by the surfing communities around Perth soon becoming synonymous with Australian surfing culture as a whole. These fleecy boots might not have looked particularly flattering, but what did that matter when you were young, toned and bronzed?

In 1978 one Australian surfer, Brian Smith, took the ugg to California, where, after a few false starts, he managed to penetrate the American surfer market. Soon after, he registered the UGG as a trademark and sold the brand on, though it was two decades or so before it finally made its mark on the fashion scene. Today this bulky but cosy boot is as much a staple of urban dress as black leggings or opaque tights sported by everyone from stars to schoolgirls. It is a relatively rare example of comfort before looks – as long as the lifestyle references and brand associations are right.

Right and below: The Australian-born UGG may be bulky and clompy, but its simple silhouette assimilates comfortably with a feminine look.

NIKE AIR JORDAN 1

1984
Nike

By the early 1980s the range of running shoes that had established Nike a decade earlier (see pages 56–7) were beginning to lose their popularity. It was clear that the Oregon-based sports shoe manufacturer needed to evolve new products aimed at new audiences with which to reinvent and revitalize itself. All too often at this time Nike was seen solely as the purveyor of 'white men's jogging shoes'.

Nike identified the emerging African-American basketball player Michael Jordan (1963–) as a potential endorser of the new shoe it came up with and, after some initial resistance, finally managed to woo him for a reputed fee of $2.5 million. Jordan began to appear at matches wearing the striking red, black and white shoe, whose telegenic looks were miles away from the all-white articles sanctioned by the National Basketball Association. NBA fines only heightened the frenzy surrounding the Air Jordan, or 'Js', and the model's long career took off.

To date there have been 23 versions of the Air Jordan, most sporting the 'Jumpman' silhouette logo of Jordan performing a balletic basketball move. The shoe has become a cultural icon and a potent tool in the transformation of Nike into a global superbrand.

Right and below: Sports superstar Michael Jordan endorsed the Air Jordan in a marketing campaign that established Nike as a global brand. The first version of the shoe was designed by Peter Moore; many of the later versions, however, were the work of Nike's cult designer Tinker Hatfield.

'WATCH' SHOE

c.1987
Red or Dead

The curiously named British fashion label Red or Dead was named in allusion to co-founder Wayne Hemmingway's Native American (in less PC terms, 'Red Indian') background. The name is equally suggestive, however, of the company's refreshingly playful approach to fashion, daring to take itself seriously without losing sight of the fun.

Husband-and-wife team Wayne (1961–) and Geraldine (1961–) Hemmingway began their business in 1982 on a secondhand clothes stall at London's Camden Lock market, but quickly expanded enough to open a shop in Kensington. Their first own-brand clothes collection was launched in 1983, with their debut shoe collection following two years later. By now Red or Dead shops had opened up across the capital, with outlets in trendsetting districts such as Soho and Covent Garden.

By the end of the decade, shoes had become the mainstay of the business, in part fuelled by the commercial success of eyecatching designs such the Watch shoe, which was famously worn by 1980s teen band Bros. Many 1980s Red or Dead shoes owe an undoubted debt to that great British staple, the chunky Dr Martens (a brand they had helped revamp), but a nice line in irony and wit transformed them into something utterly new.

Right: With its mixture of tough urban chic and playful wit, the Watch shoe helped place Red or Dead at the forefront of British street fashion in the late 1980s.

'MOCK-CROC' PLATFORMS

1993
Vivienne Westwood

If you're going to trip, do it in style. Supermodel Naomi Campbell, wearing a tartan outfit and slippery cream rubber stockings, famously fell from these blue leather 'mock-croc' 10 inch platforms at Vivienne Westwood's Anglomania autumn/winter show in 1993. Westwood's shoes – gorgeous and outrageous in equal measure – are the ultimate in fun and dressing up. Even Naomi saw the humorous side, managing to grin broadly as she toppled over.

Pioneer of punk, subverter of tradition, and arch-proclaimer of individuality, Westwood (1941–) has gained notoriety many times over since she first emerged in the mid 1970s. Not only her dresses but her bags and shoes, too, have had an enduring power to both shock and delight. The 'mock-croc' platforms encapsulate Westwood's wondrously fearless reinterpretation of fashion history, which has always been the backbone of her dynamic designs.

These platform beauties may hark back to the glorious excesses of Marie-Antoinette and the Ancien Régime. They may even have more than have a whiff of the fairytale, perfect, perhaps, for some street-savvy, brazen Cinderella. But what their intended message was to proclaim was women's freedom to experiment and their sexuality – playfully manipulating the past, but also foreshadowing things to come.

Right: Naomi Campbell slips and falls in an iconic catwalk moment wearing an iconic pair of shoes. Westwood's brightly coloured and exaggeratedly proportioned shoes are a fabulous example of her daring reinterpretation of fashion history.

HOMMAGE À GIGER

1993
René van den Berg

To work well, extravagance and innovation in design rely on an acute understanding of skills and techniques. The Dutch shoe designer René van den Berg (1964–) has just such a solid understanding – not only did he work as an orthopaedic technician before turning to custom shoe design in 1992, but behind him is a rich family tradition of shoemaking dating back more than a hundred years. His shoes may look extreme, but nonethless, as footwear, they do the job.

Van den Berg's sculptural designs fuse fashion with fine art and fetish. In this extraordinary boot – the first women's shoe he designed – he pays homage to the Swiss artist Hans Rüdi Giger (1940–), whose dark, surrealistic work is best known through his designs for the cult horror sci-fi film *Alien* (1979). Its hornlike toe, talonlike heel and ridged vamp make obvious allusion to the sickening monster of Ridley Scott's film, but the boot is also evocative of gothic fairytale – it's not hard to imagine this as the favoured footwear of the wicked queen in *Snow White*.

It comes as no surprise to discover that van den Berg is regularly commissioned to provide designs for fashion shows, music videos and theatre. He has worked with fashion designers such as Thierry Mugler, Art of Vanity and Alexander van Slobbe.

Right: Hommage à Giger formed part of René van den Berg's first shoe collection, entitled The Beauty of the Beast. With its obvious allusion to fairy tale, the collection blurred the conventional boundaries between the ugly and the beautiful.

CAMPARI 'MARY JANES'

1994
Manolo Blahnik

Manolo Blahnik is sometimes described as the fifth lead in *Sex and the City* owing to the sheer number of times his shoes are worn and hankered after by the series' fashion-obsessed characters. In one famous scene, lead character Carrie Bradshaw, newspaper columnist and out-and-out fashionista, stumbles across a pair of slender black patent shoes in a store cupboard at US *Vogue* and in awed tones proclaims, 'Oh my God. Manolo Blahnik "Mary Janes", an urban shoe myth!' Satiric, ludicrous, ironic … yes – but it's a scene that encapsulates the nigh-on mythic status that Blahnik today holds among shoe aficionados everywhere.

For all his celebrity status, Blahnik has remained resolutely down to earth – exemplified by the fact that he has always been involved at every stage of his shoes' creation – designing the prototypes, making the preliminary sketches, sculpting the wooden lasts and, finally, overseeing production. Without any formal training, he once claimed that his skill in shoemaking lay solely in he fact that he had 'the best taste in the world'. Years of trial and error led him to a successful formula for his collections – a combination of shoes with 'solid good looks that will last for ever' and a few more adventurous pieces for the daring and wealthy.

The 'Mary Janes' in question are actually called Campari shoes and, in spite of being a model that is more than ten years old, they are still being manufactured to satisfy constant demand.

Right: A 'Manolo' has become slang for any desirable, eye-wincingly expensive shoe. The Campari, made iconic by *Sex and the City*, is among the most coveted of Blahnik's designs.

PELOTA

1995
Camper

When, in 1995, the Spanish footwear company Camper issued the first examples of its Pelota range, it found it had hit upon a successful formula for urban footwear – a shoe with all the informality of the athletics trainer but without the ostentatious styling that characterizes so many of the street-fashion brands. Here was a shoe in most cases respectable enough to wear at work, but stylish enough to show off at play. Camper, in short, had discovered the middle ground … and struck gold.

Camper itself was formed as long ago as 1975 – the first store opened in Barcelona in 1981 – but it was not until the 1990s that it gained a European profile, with stores launched in the continent's trendsetting capitals – London, Paris, Milan. The Pelota was conceived as a key player in this onward expansion. Styled in the vein of a bowling shoe, the Pelota has an affable feel – neutral earthy hues and a slightly bulbous toe result in an easy compromise between macho sportiness and feminine softness that is well suited to the modern metrosexual male.

Is this, then, the perfect footwear for our times? It is certainly a contender. Versatile, comfortable and with just the right degree of quirkiness, the Pelota provides one great advantage for the average city-dwelling man – once bought, there is no need to worry about what to wear on your feet and no need to go shopping again … That is, at least, until your current favourite pair wears out.

Right: This sporty sensible shoe fast became the favoured footwear for men seeking an understated, nonconfrontational style. Below: The distinctive bubbly sole of the Pelota.

MBT

1996
Karl Müller

MBT stands for Masai Barefoot Technology, but this distinctive shoe did not simply spring ready-formed out of Africa. The design was invented by the Swiss engineer and former athlete Karl Müller who, while walking barefoot across a soft Korean paddy field, noticed how the pain caused by his knee, back and Achilles tendon problems seemed to lessen. Further research showed that members of the Masai tribe in Kenya, who mainly walk shoeless, hardly ever suffer from back pain and are renowned for their upright, graceful posture.

With its heelless curved rubber sole, the MBT is meant to replicate the rocking motion of walking across soft ground even when used on hard surfaces like city pavements. Originally conceived as a remedial shoe, the MBT really only became popular when fitness fans discovered that the additional muscular effort required to walk 'like a Masai' also had the bonus of toning the buttocks, thighs and calf muscles. Even standing still in MBTs requires work – almost like balancing on a rubber ball.

The MBT may have become a Hollywood must-have, but debate still rages about its health benefits. What is clear, though, is that the MBT represents a significant challenge to conventional shoe design – from an ergonomic, not fashion, perspective.

Right: The MBT may look like a hybrid of the traditional sports shoe, but it was conceived to replicate the natural rocking motion of the foot when walking barefoot and to capitalize on the attendant health benefits.

FEATHER-TRIMMED SHOE

1998
Jimmy Choo

Ever since a 1998 episode of *Sex and the City*, the Jimmy Choo brand has had a status in popular culture that must be the envy of fashion businesses the world over. Who can forget the hilarious moment – and tongue-in-cheek pun – when footwear queen Carrie Bradshaw (yes, her again!), in a mad dash for a ferry, trips over and loses one of her lilac-suede feather-trimmed shoes? 'Wait!' she screams, 'I've lost my Choo!' Almost overnight, it seemed, Jimmy Choo became a sensation and in the following years no Oscar night seemed complete without an elegant, sparkling pair of his shoes on the red carpet.

Who would have predicted the brand's meteoric rise when, in 1986, the Malaysian-born designer Jimmy Choo Yeang Keat (1961–) set up his handmade shoe business in Hackney, a then little-known impoverished district of metropolitan London? The refinement and meticulous craft of his products soon won him attention – notably an unprecedented four-spread feature in British *Vogue* in 1988 – but it was only in 1996, after he teamed up with Tamara Mellon (1967–), the accessories editor at *Vogue*, that the Jimmy Choo brand went global, concentrating on ready-to-wear lines that were largely produced in Italy.

In 2001 Choo sold his share in his namesake company to concentrate on what he does best – the creation of glamorous yet wearable handmade shoes of superlative design and craftsmanship.

Right: The lilac-suede feather-trimmed shoe lost by Carrie Bradshaw in *Sex and the City* – a lovely example of Jimmy Choo's gorgeously feminine designs.

EIN/TRITT SHOE

2000s
Catherine Meuter

As most people know, origami is the traditional Japanese art of paper folding, and its influence is obvious in these elegant geometric shoes designed by Catherine Meuter. The ready-cut shoe comes flat-packed and is easy to assemble, while the material is reinforced in parts so as to provide the necessary rigidity and durability when worn.

In form, of course, these are another example of the 'heel-less high heels' popularized by designers such as Antonio Berardi (see pages 80–81) and United Nude. For some, the architectonic style may seem too obvious, too rigid. But the EIN/TRITT remains at present a conceptual prototype and its importance lies, above all, in the challenge it lays down to traditional forms of manufacture and the new directions it opens up in the evolving story of shoe design.

Clearly Meuter's design has obvious advantages in terms of cutting transportation and storage costs – perfect for our environmentally anxious age – but it is perhaps its playful interactivity that taps into a deeper trend, engaging the end-user as an active participant in the making process. Undoubtedly, this is a prototype that will bear fruit in the years to come.

Right: In spite of its unorthodox method of assembly, the EIN/TRITT shoe does not compromise on style. Below: Front and back views of the innovative prototype shoe.

EXTREME BALLERINA HEELS 2   c.2000

Christian Louboutin

The French designer Christian Louboutin's (1964–) choice of career was reputedly based on his fascination with the costumes of Parisian showgirls whom he used to watch in clubs while playing truant from school. For him, the high heel was the ultimate embellishment of the female body, emphasizing the slenderness and sheerness of the leg.

Sexuality and transmutation are superabundant in Louboutin's Extreme Ballerina Heels 2, which combine the high heel with another common fetish object – the pointe ballet shoe. Both genres of footwear have strong associations with constriction and pain – high heels compress the toes, make the feet ache and, in some instances, can cause long-term health problems; ballerinas can suffer agonies while performing the daily routine of pointework. The fusion of the two creates a startling design that exposes the sadomasochism that can underlie women's fashion.

Despite the radicalism of such creations, Louboutin is today one of the most sought-after of contemporary shoe designers. His more conventional designs – sexy, yes, but lyrical and wearable, too – have graced the feet of Angelina Jolie, Kylie Minogue and Britney Spears. It's not hard to spot them – just watch out for those trademark crimson soles, inspired by an employee's nail polish.

Right: Extreme design – Christian Louboutin's startling piece of footwear marries the high heel and the pointe shoe to excruciating effect. Its overt fetishism recalls the iconic shoe-sculpture of Méret Oppenheim (see pages 20–21).

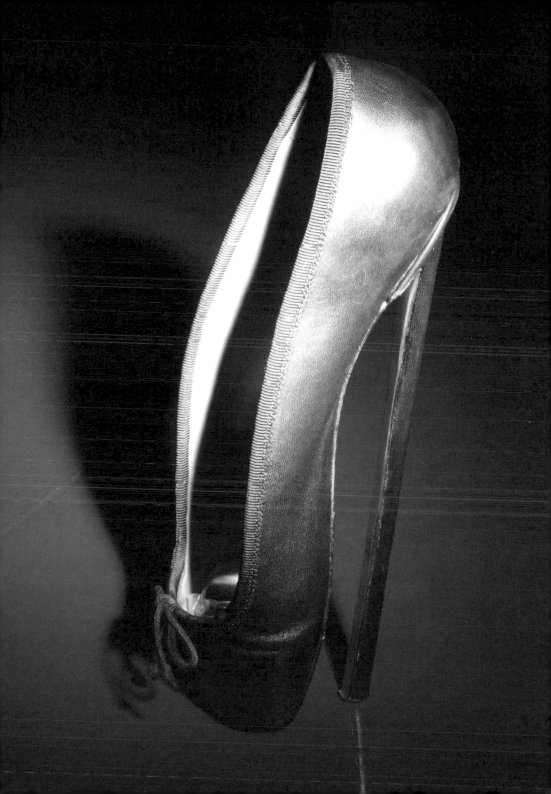

HEELLESS BOOT

c.2000
Antonio Berardi

These boots take to an extreme the elongation of the woman's body usually associated with the dizzying heights of heeled shoes. Like a castrated stiletto, the heelless boot combines poise with vulnerability. Restricting balance, constricting movement and forcing a painful posture, it 'de-emancipates' in the style of bygone corsetry. For all that, this teetering, balletic look offers great red-carpet opportunities … as Victoria Beckham and Gwyneth Paltrow have shown.

Their designer is the Italian-English couturier Antonio Berardi (1968–), whose powerful, geometric dress designs have drawn comparison with the work of near-contemporaries such as Alexander McQueen and Hussein Chalayan. Heelless shoes and boots are by no means new, but they have undergone something of a radical revival in the new millennium, with examples by Kei Kagami (see pages 100–01) and United Nude among others. It's a style that has attracted much comment, but the experimental, theatrical flamboyance it evinces is a healthy ingredient in any design industry.

Right and below: This ironic take on glamorous boots shows to what lengths people will go to look supremely chic.

80

JOE SNEAKER

c.2000
Emma Hope

Emma Hope (1962–) was part of a particularly rich generation of talented shoe designers that emerged in Britain in the mid to late 1980s. Like many of her peers – Patrick Cox and Jimmy Choo among them – she attended the prestigious Cordwainers College (now part of the London College of Fashion) in Hackney, East London. Early in her career she designed collections for Laura Ashley, Betty Jackson and Jean Muir, before launching her own brand and store in 1987.

Emma Hope's designs have become collectibles, perhaps none more so than the Joe Sneaker. Despite its name, this is essentially a feminine interpretation of the traditional sneaker – one that lays down a challenge to the supposedly androgynous styling of its forebear. While the thick sole, white toe and white laces may be reminiscent of the Converse All-Star (see pages 16–17), the elegant, narrow shape alludes to that most feminine of footwear, the ballerina flat. The delicately patterned uppers, too, also subvert the masculine, even macho, heritage of the typical Nike or Reebok shoe.

There is room in the world for a relaxed comfortable style that it also a bit girly and a bit glam. Hope has described her shoes as 'foot regalia' – and the Joe Sneaker richly deserves that appellation.

Right and below: Variations in colour and texture of the sensible women's shoe that still manages to be feminine in spite of its sneaker heritage.

VIVO BAREFOOT

Like the MBT (see pages 72–3), the Vivo Barefoot range is an attempt to design shoes that replicate the experience of walking barefoot, but in this case the emphasis is on the sensory contact between foot and ground.

A great deal of scientific research would suggest that it is much healthier not to wear shoes at all and that the constricting or deforming features of many shoe designs, such as high heels, platforms or narrow, pointed toes, can radically alter natural muscular movement throughout the body. With hundreds of thousands of nerve endings, moreover, feet are designed to act as ultra-sensitive receptors, sending complex series of messages to the brain that inform balance and how the body should react and move. However, the conventional emphasis on aesthetics in shoe design has thwarted the ancient harmony between sole and soil.

Tim Brennan (1977–) first came up with the idea for the Vivo in 2001, while an MA student at the Royal College of Art. Together with the Clarks-owned company Terra Plana, he developed a puncture-resistant ultra-thin sole for a shoe that aimed to minimize the interface between the wearer and the ground. The product was eventually launched in 2003.

Right: The understated styling of this shoe gives away little about its ergonomic, health-promoting design, most significantly its puncture-resistant sole.
Below: Extra width in the toe helps stimulate natural movement in the foot.

CROCS

From time to time the humble, unassuming clog thuds its way onto the fashion radar. A current manifestation is the Croc, a brightly coloured plastic shoe that has no pretensions to either elegance or trendiness but which, for all that, has won a worldwide following – drawn by its cheapness, disposability and outright fun.

Crocs were launched as outdoor boating shoes in 2002, but soon slipped their moorings to become an all-out cult. With their childlike colours, chunky looks and lightweight feel, they rapidly caught on as an indoor/outdoor, anytime/anywhere shoe for the young and old, grungy and groovy. Some fans like to purchase a Crocs style such as the Beach in every one of its 20-odd rainbow colours.

Even the big ventilation holes seem to have caught the public's imagination – one company, Jibbitz (quickly acquired by Crocs, Inc.), issues plastic accessories such as flowers and butterflies that wearers can fix into the holes and, in so doing, customize their shoes.

Right: The new flip-flops? A pair of easy-to-wear, durable and washable plastic Crocs.

ALEX SHOE

2003
Maiko Dawson

Handmade shoes are generally considered an extravagant luxury. On the other hand, in an age saturated by the mass-produced and the lowest common denominator, it is reassuring to discover that there are still designers who are practising a traditional craft while at the same time engaging with contemporary sensibilities.

The Japanese-born, London-based Maiko Dawson (1970–) is just such a designer. Like many of her British peers, she is a graduate of the prestigious Cordwainers College in Hackney, East London and set up her own workshop in the city in the late 1990s. She adopted traditional shoemaking methods partly because of her concern with environmentalism but also because she believes that good-quality materials and attention to detail are what make footwear both beautiful and comfortably functional. The natural world is the primary inspiration for her organic, pared-down shoes, which are often presented in earthen hues.

The two-tone Alex shoe is exemplary of her approach. Its sophisticatedly simple form is contemporary enough to be relevant and desirable but nonetheless remains aloof from passing fads. This is a shoe that suggests exclusivity and individuality quietly, but without resorting to ostentatious wackiness.

Independent designers play a key role in any design industry. If new ideas and new blood are to flow, these stand-alone figures need to be nurtured, treasured and preserved.

Right: The simply styled and exquisitely made Alex shoe by London-based designer Maiko Dawson is a fine example of understated bespoke design.

BIRKENSTOCK SANDAL

In 2002 the Hollywood actress Gwyneth Paltrow was photographed walking around London in a pair of Birkenstock sandals. Seeming at first a footwear faux-pas, it startled commentators by fuelling a fashion frenzy, and 2003 saw panic buying of the wholesome no-frills shoe to the extent that some retailers decided to restrict customers to one pair per purchase. 'Birks', it seemed, were back with a vengeance.

The Birkenstock sandal, of course, has been around for a long time, inextricably associated with hippies, vegetarians and every kind of countercultural refusenik. The origins of the brand can be traced back to eighteenth-century Germany, but the homey sandal as we know it was first produced in 1964, when Karl Birkenstock (1937–) developed the first flexible arch support suitable for mass manufacture. The sandal's claims to podiatric virtue initially made it popular as footwear among German health professionals – initially hard to break in, the shoe is said to mould itself to the individual's foot shape and gait. The perfect method of self-customization, you could say.

For all its supposed frumpiness and do-goody associations, it is the simplicity of the Birkenstock that appeals to the current generation of wearers. Worn with socks it might be somewhat beyond the pale, but with blue jeans and feet open to the world it's a classic, unassuming style.

Right: No frills – three variations of the wholesome Birkenstock that have stepped forth into mainstream fashion in recent years. Classic features are the cork footbed and the plain, chunky straps and buckles.

CUPS ELK

Radical design sometimes requires the invention of a new visual language. Trippen is a German brand of shoes that has achieved this tricky task with skill and confident flair. The company was established in 1992 by Angela Spieth and Michael Oehler, whose first show, held in a Berlin art gallery, consisted of 60 innovative wooden shoes, some wearable, some unwearable. The first Trippen shop opened in 1995, with others swiftly following across Europe and in Japan.

At the core of the Trippen ethos is a belief in socially responsible, environmentally sensitive design, coupled with a determination to create strongly individual shoes that transcend mainstream fashion trends. Trippen produces shoes in large, evolving collections – such as Cups, x + os and Penna – based around unchanging components such as lasts and sole units. Creativity thus becomes a highly important ingredient in the development of original, eyecatching 'variations on a theme'.

Cups Elk is a subgenre of the ongoing Cups collection, making use of a somewhat unusual material in modern shoe design – soft elk leather – though traditionally, of course, it was widely used by the native peoples of North America and northern Europe. Tradition and innovation, comfort and style, are ingeniously allied.

Right: Three variations of the Cups Elk shoe showing something of the versatility of its innovatively designed components. Below: An aerial view that makes clear the clever combination of traditional form and innovative detailing.

THE NAT-2 SHOE

c.2003
K&T

The convertible shoe has arrived. With the aid of a zip that follows the plimsoll line of a traditional-looking sneaker, the upper can be unfastened and removed to reveal a sandal hidden beneath.

This ingenious two-in-one shoe is said to have been conceived by designer Stephen Yeung when he was packing for a trip. Why waste space in a suitcase, he thought, when the shoes you are wearing could be made to adapt into other styles of footwear? Yeung realized his new concept, the Nat-2 shoe, in collaboration with Matthias and Sebastian Thies of the German company K&T and today some 20 styles are available in the range.

To some tastes, the result may seem gimmicky, but the exuberant styling more than compensates. Funky colours and electic patterns emphasize the playful qualities of the shoe – who, after all, can resist the childish joys of unzipping and zipping and, as if by magic, transforming – even in a small way – the world around us?

Right: Two for the price of one – this sneaker-styled shoe unzips to reveal a strappy sandal alternative.

SPEED STILETTO

2007
Pierre Hardy

The Speed Stiletto is a hybrid shoe that celebrates the schizophrenic, postmodern mixing and matching of recent fashion trends. In a joyfully preposterous *jeu d'esprit*, the French designer Pierre Hardy has placed an athletics shoe on an arched sole supported by a tall stiletto heel, thereby combining contradictory visual statements of enhanced and hampered movement within a single cohesive design.

Such eclecticism comes naturally to Hardy, who launched his own label in 1999. Initially trained in the fine arts, he plunders a dazzling array of references when creating his collections – from Renaissance master Sandro Botticelli to postmodern guru Ettore Sottsass. His work rides roughshod, too, over conventional notions of high and low – he is quite as able to design for historic fashion house Balenciaga (for whom he created the celebrated Open-toed Cage sandal of 2001) as for a high-street multinational such as Gap.

The Speed Stiletto is just such an encounter between high and low – in more senses than just one. Its function, of course, is not to make it possible to run in high-heeled shoes, but rather to suggest that a dressed-down style can also be impeccably glamorous.

Right: Lifestyle statements collide in this sporty high-heeled shoe by French designer Pierre Hardy.

ELECTRIC LIGHT SHOE

2008
ASICS/Onitsuka Tiger

The athletics shoe holds a seemingly unassailable position in today's global fashion industry and the market is dominated, if not saturated, by a handful of powerful US or European brands – Adidas, Nike and Reebok among them. Smaller, and especially, non-US or non-EU companies have a tough act on their hands to try to muscle in. The Electric Light Shoe is one such company's ingenious attempt to share in the limelight.

Onitsuka is older than both Nike and Reebok and almost contemporary with Adidas. Established in Japan in 1949, it was the first Japanese company to produce basketball shoes. Over the decades, it gradually raised its international profile and became particularly associated with the cross-stripes design that first appeared in its Mexico 66 shoe. In 1977 Onitsuka merged with other Japanese sports companies to form ASICS – an acronym of the well-known Latin tag *anima sana in corpore sano* ('a healthy mind in a healthy body'). Onitsuka Tiger, however, remained ASICS's premier international brand.

In 2008, as part of its ongoing attempts to strengthen its global position, Onitsuka Tiger launched a marketing campaign called 'Electric Tiger Land'. Its centrepiece – commissioned from the Dutch design company Freedom of Creation – is a spectacular, one-metre-long illuminated shoe whose body is made up of a bewilderingly intricate cityscape. Superhighways appear as the famous cross-stripes and the city's buildings as a kaleidoscope of Japanese signs and symbols.

City and technology, nation and iconic shoe, have coalesced in a single, shimmering sculpture. It is a potent salvo in the ongoing struggle to break the superbrands' hegemony in athletic footwear design.

Right: Made of Japan – the Electric Light Shoe is a shimmering reclamation of the athletics shoe as a Japanese article. Below: One of the hundreds of intricate components that make up the shoe.

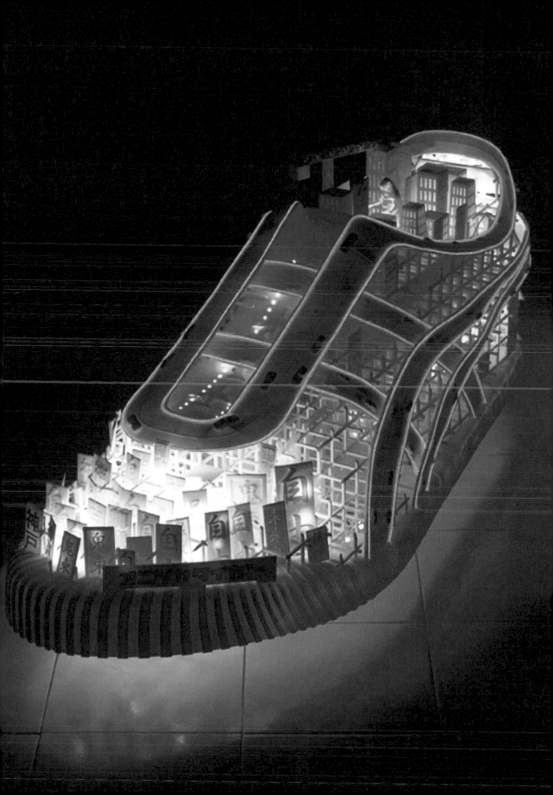

The Japanese-born designer Kei Kagami has an impeccable pedigree – at the close of the 1980s he worked as a studio assistant for John Galliano and in 1992 he graduated alongside Alexander McQueen from the prestigious London design college Central St Martins. Perhaps his closest kindred spirit, however, is Hussein Chalayan, with whom he shares an experimental, questioning spirit and a desire to transcend the conventional boundaries of fashion. A dress made entirely of wax and another from a carpet of living cress have been among creations that have by turns delighted and perplexed the fashion press.

Kagami launched his own couture label in 2000. A major shoe collection followed two years later, when it was displayed much like a sculpture exhibition at a gallery in Milan. Featuring layered compositions, unexpected materials and gravity-defying forms, Kagami's shoes display his plastic imagination at its best as he strives to realize his dreamlike ideas in a fusion of engineering and sculpture. Sometimes the results may seem whimsical, but there is always the sense that Kagami has set out to redefine what a shoe can and should be.

Innovation in design often flows from development in technology and the availability of new materials. At other times, however, things move forward through a seemingly maverick and playful approach that turns tradition on its head to create a new set of rules and boundaries.

Right: Early in his career, Kagami became associated with rather ponderous, architectonic heels. In recent years he has tried to lessen the importance of the heel – as in this design from 2008 – or to deny it altogether, as in the heelless designs of 2009.

MEDIC ESTHETIC

2008
Gwendolyn Huskens

Conventionally, shoe design aims to promote perfection, to transform the humble foot into an object of desire. Shoes should be sleek and sensual, beautiful and artful … and yes, if possible, comfortable, too.

It is this paradigm that recent graduate Gwendolyn Huskens radically subverted in her graduation show at Eindhoven's Academy of Art in the Netherlands. In her six-piece collection Medic Esthetic, each of the shoes or boots alludes to orthopaedic footwear or to some other kind of medical intervention. One sinuous boot is made out of bandages, another takes the form of a plastercast … The traditional materials of the shoe designer are discarded for the 'unsightly' ones of medicine – stainless steel, Band-Aids, fibreglass and plaster of paris; conventional, streamlined forms for bulky heels and ugly buckles, intrusive braces and straps.

In creating her shoes, Huskens sought to draw attention to some of the taboos surrounding physical imperfection, deformity and disability usually left off the agenda of mainstream fashion, and, in so doing, to challenge the often frivolous and decadent nature of footwear fashion. For all that, however, her creations achieve a surprising, if surreal, beauty all of their own.

Right: Medical materials are transformed into the surreally beautiful in these shoes and boots by the Dutch designer Gwendolyn Huskens.

MELISSA ANGLOMANIA

2008
Vivienne Westwood

The Brazilian manufacturer Melissa is renowned for its innovative use of injection-moulded plastic to create playful, adventurous shoe and accessory designs. In recent times, as part of its strategy, the company has courted high-profile collaborations with leading international design figures including the Campana brothers, the architect Zaha Hadid (see pages 106–08) and that much-loved maverick of the catwalk, Vivienne Westwood.

The Anglomania range that Westwood has designed for Melissa evokes the classic, hyperfeminine glamour of the 1950s. With their dynamic silhouettes, intense flat colour and flamboyant logo, these shoes are unapologetically plastic yet gorgeous and special nonetheless. The qualities of a cheap and transient material are celebrated rather than shamefacedly disguised. These are shoes to be worn proudly and defiantly, with the rebellious, subversive spirit so closely associated with Westwood.

The Anglomania range may not mould around the foot or resist wear and tear in the way their leather counterparts might. But does this matter? Worn to an occasional party or as an integral part of a feel-good outfit, they will always radiate individualism and glamour. This is testament to great and sensitive design that surpasses the need for precious materials and traditional craft skills.

Right: These fantastically plastic shoes designed by Vivienne Westwood for Melissa have catwalk glamour but are affordable enough to be fun for all.

MELISSA SHOE

The Iraqi-born, London-based architect Zaha Hadid (1950–) is today well known for her innovative works such as the Vitra fire station in Weil am Rhein, Germany, or the Bridge Pavilion in Zaragoza, Spain. Less well known, however, is her track record of diversification into other design disciplines. From furniture to cars and fashion design, Hadid applies her intuitive, dynamic aesthetic to whatever she creates.

Hadid's first foray into shoe design was in collaboration with the Brazilian footwear manufacturer Melissa (see pages 104–05). This fluid, asymmetrical shoe revisits many of Hadid's architectural and spatial interests on a small scale and attempts to introduce a fresh urgency and dynamism into footwear design. These are shoes to be seen in movement, not static in a window display. Like Hadid's buildings, too, the design is the product of computer-based ergonomic research and prototyping – which is, perhaps, what gives the shoes their suggestion of being almost 'virtual', of being hardly real at all.

The following year, 2009, also saw the launch of another Hadid shoe design – this time for the French clothing company Lacoste.

Right: Architecture meets shoe design – fluid lines and organic forms make Zaha Hadid's shoe for Melissa seem as unfeasibly light and aerodynamic as one of her world-renowned buildings.

INDEX

PICTURE CREDITS

The publisher would like to thank the following contributors for their kind permission to reproduce the following photographs:

2 Dr Martens; 7 Freedom of Creation; 9 Fox Photos/Getty Images; 11 Bettmann/Corbis; 12 Henry Groskinsky/Time & Life Pictures/Getty Images; 13 Timothy H. O'Sullivan/ Hulton Archive/Getty Images; 15 Gene Lester/Getty Images; 16 ©The Andy Warhol Foundation for the Visual Arts/Corbis; 17 Paul Natkin/ WireImage; 19 Museo Salvatore Ferragamo; 21 ©Meret Oppenheim/Moderna Museet, Stockholm; 23 Museo Salvatore Ferragamo; 24 & 25 MGM/The Kobal Collection; 27 V&A Images/ Victoria & Albert Museum; 28 & 29 Dr Martens; 31 Clarks; 33 Tods Group; 35 akg-images; 36 & 37 Hush Puppies Europe/Wolverine Worldwide Inc; 39 Sonny Meddle/Rex Features; 40 & 41 Dr Martens; 42 Popperfoto/Getty Images; 43 Keystone-France/Eyedea/ Camera Press London; 45 Popperfoto/Getty Images; 47 Paulo Fridman/Corbis; 48 & 49 Tods Groups; 51 Manolo Blahnik; 53 V&A Images/Victoria & Albert Museum; 54 Helene Rogers/ Alamy; 55 Jose Azel/Aurora/ Getty Images; 56 & 57 Nike; 58 Humberto Carreno/Rex Features; 59 Camera Press/ More/BCM; 60 Focus on Sport/Getty Images; 61 Nathaniel S. Butler/NBAE/ Getty Images; 63 Red or Dead; 65 Niall McInerney; 67 Rene van den Berg; 69 Manolo Blahnik; 70 & 71 Camper UK; 73 MBT; 75 Jimmy Choo; 76 & 77 Nici Jost/Catherine Meuter; 79 Christian Louboutin; 80 & 81 Karl Prouse/Catwalking/ Getty Images; 82 & 83 Emma Hope; 84 & 85 Terra Plana; 87 Realimage/Alamy; 89 Maiko Dawson; 91 The Boot Tree Ltd/Birkenstock; 92 & 93 Trippen; 95 K&T; 97 Pierre Hardy; 98 & 99 Freedom of Creation; 101 Enamul Hoque; 103 Rene van der Hulst; 105 Melissa/ Vivienne Westwood; 107 Zaha Hadid.

Every effort has been made to trace the copyright holders and we apologise in advance for any unintentional errors or omissions, and would be pleased to insert the appropriate acknowledgment in any subsequent publication.

CREDITS

First published in 2009
by Conran Octopus Ltd
a part of Octopus Publishing
Group, 2–4 Heron Quays
London E14 4JP
www.octopusbooks.co.uk

An Hachette Livre UK
Company
www.hachettelivre.co.uk

Distributed in the United
States and Canada by
Octopus Books USA, c/o
Hachette Book Group USA,
237 Park Avenue, New York,
NY 10017 USA

British Library Cataloguing-
in-Publication Data.
A catalogue record for
this book is available
from the British Library.

Text written by:
Michael Czerwinski

Publisher:
Lorraine Dickey
Consultant Editor:
Deyan Sudjic
Managing Editor:
Sybella Marlow
Editor:
Robert Anderson

Art Director:
Jonathan Christie
Design:
Untitled
Picture Researcher:
Anne-Marie Hoines

Production Manager:
Katherine Hockley
Production Controller:
Pauline Le Navenec

ISBN: 978 1 84091 539 6
Printed in China